The
Book
of
BIG Thoughts

By Karen Anderson

Volume 5

TABLE OF CONTENTS

NOTE:

Some of the chapters address satan, the chief evil-doer. As he is the lowest of the low, he is not given the courtesy of a capital letter on his name unless it appears as the first word in the sentence.

Oceans of Life
Return to Life

"...together in life, together in death..."
2 Samuel 1:23

I sit here by a roaring fire at beautiful Marine Dunes, just north of Monterey, California. As I look out over God's beautiful ocean, I reflect on His vision for me and what He has planned for my life. The sky and ocean are blue, the roar of the waves, and the wind blowing, I am overwhelmed as I watch and ponder about the glory and majesty of what God has done for me. But first let's reflect on the ocean and all its wonders.

The ocean has always been the strength for my life. I relate my life to the ocean and this is why, when there is turmoil, my first response is, "Take me to the ocean!" This will bring balance to the turmoil in my life. Visualize with me sitting on the ocean shore and seeing the vastness of the sea which stretches beyond the horizons. There seems to be no end in sight, just that elusive line that keeps going further and further out of reach. I wonder, "Is there land over there out of my sight?" "Who lives there?" "Do they have the same questions about their future as I do about mine?" Even as I wonder, I am at peace. The ocean reminds me of the majesty of God and how He is never ending and always there and I can depend on Him. What peace and comfort that brings to my life! This is why the ocean is "life" to me. I feel balance and peace when I am sitting on the seashore...*I FEEL HIM!*

Here I sit on the sandy shores realizing the consistency of God's great ocean. When you watch the movement of the tide, the crashing of the surf going in and out without stopping...have you noticed...the waves never give up. You can see the tremendous effort as each wave strives to reach the shore. Will the wave finally reach the shore and deposit the gifts it has to share with me?

I have a vision in those times of struggle, loneliness, and despair that may help you too. Imagine you are standing on the high rocks by the ocean side. You have a large apron on and the waves are coming at you higher and higher. Open your apron wide and accept the gift that is being given to you. Imagine when the waves come, instead of waves of water (which would still be a blessing) there are millions of roses which represent love coming your way. God is showering you with His love and blessings. Through this vision I am receiving the gifts the waves have for me.

There are other JOYS at the ocean shore. It always tickles my soul when I feel the water from the wave come up under my feet and then as it flows back into the ocean, pulling the sand out from under my feet. It makes me feel giddy. I remember watching my dog when the same thing would happen. She would get so excited she would take off running like crazy. What fun! I love the shock of the cold water as it washes over my bare feet. Or hearing someone shouting, "Watch out!" At that point I just can't move fast enough and sure enough I am soaked up to my knees...sand everywhere. Again, what fun!

What fun it is to walk along the seashore looking for those sea shells, or even other unexpected delights. I remember at one of the California beaches my husband found a rock formation with hundreds of tiny crabs running through the rocks. Or what about that perfect rock formation that you had never seen before. On our trip to St. Marteen in the Caribbean, there was a small island called Sand Island...very small for an island but there were some of the most interesting rocks that were actually formed by the sand. The sand would form itself around an object like a sea creature's discarded shell, or around a twig. It was amazing some of the shapes and mysteries that could be found and admired. Remember everything is of God. It is His majesty and splendor we were witnessing and you too probably have seen such wonders.

There are wonders beyond our understanding under the sea, and they are magnificent in God's eyes. There are wonders above the waves that are magnificent too. I love watching the lights, at night, that are coming from the ships and lighthouses. They are always showing you the way to safe travels. Isn't that the way God wants to help you in your life? I personally want to watch for His lights because I know I will be guided through the rough times. He will also bring me peace in those times of turbulent waters. You know the type of ocean agitation that could swamp a ship? The point is to stay the course and God's lighthouse will lead you into many exciting adventures and help you through the storms.

This leads to a personal experience where once again, God took the wonders in my life, like the ocean's gifts, but this time they did not make it to the shore. Instead it waited out in the ocean-blue for His timing and then the gift returned. I am talking about relationships. The ocean's consistency and faithfulness is God's example to us of our everyday and special relationships.

It is amazing to me the wonders all around me like the ocean, but I just don't see it until it's gone. I took what we had so much for granted. In this life...NOTHING SHOULD BE TAKEN FOR GRANTED! God has revealed His love for me more than once but several years ago, my prayers had been answered beyond my wildest dreams. I had been praying for someone in my life; that no matter what would be happening, good or bad, she would get me back on track. You know that really TRUE FRIEND that can read your every thought and emotion, and understand your fears and dreams. I am talking… **SOUL SISTER.**

At one time, I had such a person in my life but it was stolen from me through evil doings. I had been pleading with God that He would again give me a true friend. Little did I know that He had something better than finding someone new, it was bringing my SOUL SISTER back! Little would I have thought that God had a special person for my life! I truly believe that God originally brought us together knowing that we both were missing a very important part of what He wanted for us. Her name is Debra-Diane and she is God's ultimate gift to the missing side of me.

We met back in 1978 when my family was led to Corvallis, Oregon. We thought we were going there for my husband's continued education. During the 10 years, I realized we were there for a much deeper reason. The main reason for me was to find my "Soul Sister." You see, I had never experienced that extreme close relationship until I met Debra. I really didn't know what I was missing.

I first saw her smiling face, which put me at ease, at an employment agency. Through the agency I started working for a national bank as the secretary for the loan processing department. After a short time, I started receiving little notes attached to the loan papers that would come from another local bank. To my delight, the person sending the notes was Debra. We started our relationship with meeting for lunch once in a while. The funny thing was that the bank she worked for was across the street from my bank. Talk about easy access to a new budding relationship. Our friendship grew to the point that we were not only meeting for lunch during the week but we would meet at each others' home for a time of food, fun, and that **sooo** precious girl time.

We also discovered we liked the same things like cooking GREAT foods, crafts, and music to say the least. You see she was the organist and I was the pianist. We actually spent time making crafts and her family took beautiful undersea pictures that were amazing. We decided, one year to enter a craft fair with our goods, at my husband's work. I don't remember if we made a lot of money, but who cared...it was the fun of being together. I found myself wanting to be around her more and more because of her ability to always look beyond anything negative and take that next step...plus she was always smiling or laughing. I needed that in our relationship because I was serious enough for both of us. I believe the other reason we took to each other was neither of us had any pre-judgment of the other. What a blessing to be accepted unconditionally for who you are...this is a true example of unconditional love.

There may have been those that thought our relationship was perfect. The answer to this is no...but we would make fun of our differences. The only reality we knew was that we dearly loved each other. Disagreements were not going to tear us apart. I knew, from a family issue many years ago, that something small could end it. In my family because of a disagreement between my grandmother and great aunt, they did not talk with each other for the rest of their lives...that was over 40 years. There was no way I would ever let this happen with Debra and I. To keep our relationship healthy we never let our anger last long. The relationship was far too precious for us to be separated. We were always willing to do what it took to set everything right.

It is important to understand how God has everything planned even though we may not see the purpose for it. There may even be a time where you might blame God for your misfortune or the changes in your life versus what God really and truly wants for you. As I said earlier God had a definite plan for both of us.

It was fun to realize that we were the same age. A few years later we rejoiced that each of our families was having a new addition...BOYS. My son was adopted and Debra was right there giving me a baby shower while she was expecting her son. We wanted so much to grow old together. We wanted our sons to be close friends and the two families to be as close as if we were one family. To our disappointment this was not to be.

My husband and I realized in 1988 that God was calling us back to California. We had been praying for the last several months about where God was leading us. In our own lives we were dealing with a young child and an ailing grandfather who did not have the opportunity to see his grandson but a couple of times a year. God was calling us home because of my father.

I was heart sick at the idea of leaving my "soul sister" but my comfort was, I could talk with her on the phone, write letters, have visits either in Oregon or in California, and that would have to do until we could be together again.

There is no point to spend a lot of time about this portion of the story but here are a few details. For the first few months after we arrived in California I would receive a brief letter or email and maybe a much awaited short phone call...but something was wrong. She warned me about things that could not be said and if she disappeared there was information with the police. What was I to think? This was my soul sister. I wanted so desperately to find out what was going on...I needed to be there for her but my hands were tied.

I was in the dark, not knowing if she was even still alive. All I could do was pray for her and send my positive thoughts her way. I didn't even dare send a card. What drama would it cause her to have to endure? I didn't want to be the creator of that...so I prayed and thought about my "soul sister" in silence.

Praise God, that He protected her through an abusive and unfaithful life with her now ex-husband. I am so thankful that He gave Debra the strength to follow His leading and get out of that situation. I love her so much and she deserves everything God has waiting for her.

To my great surprise in early April 2010, I received a very happy email that she was back and would I like to get connected again?! I was so excited that we set the first phone conversation just a few days later. When we spoke that first day it was like the years had passed away. During the next month, we laughed and she helped me prepare for an event that was away from home. She was so helpful in the preparation, but the biggest thrill was I saw her again and could wrap my arms around her. THANK YOU GOD! The **agonizing 22-year silence was broken once** and for all...this will NEVER happen again. **THIS WAS A MIRACLE! My sister is back! We shall never part again!**

Our relationship, being returned, reminds me of the ocean waves constantly striving to reach the shore. It is a never-ending battle but with God leading, even in the times of not knowing, it is not so scary. I think about being on the seashore once again watching as the beautiful sunset drops behind the horizon. Even in that darkness you still hear the roar of the ocean waves and know the battle still continues. This reminds me of the relationship Debra and I have had over the years. Even when she was out of my sight, in the darkness, I knew that God was carrying her through the raging storms in her life and finally bringing her back into mine—**God was leading.**

Like the ocean...all through the night and day the tide continues to struggle and fight against all odds to return. Remember how the ocean is rough in a storm, churning and boiling, and tossing everything about till there is no rest. Once that stormy moment breaks, the waves slow, the foam subsides and all is calm and serene again. When you wake to a beautiful sunrise, remember God's glory and promise of a BRIGHT new day. God is there to help you live a life of JOY. Having a "soul friend" is His way of giving you someone physical you can hold onto.

God Word says, ✝ *"Two are better than one, because they have a good return for their work: if one falls down, his friend can help him up. But pity the man who falls and has no one to help him up! Also, if two lie down together, they will keep warm. But how can one keep warm alone? Though one may be overpowered, two can defend themselves. A cord of three strands if not quickly broken."* I love this verse and I know that the third strand that keeps Debra and me together is God. It was His plan for us, because we are truly "soul sisters" now and forever more!

BUT--No matter your situation…God is your ultimate "soul friend."

Do you realize that these magnificent happenings are from our Lord and Master? He wants the best for you!

✝Ecclesiastes 4:9-12 (NIV)

Protected by His Armor

Protection

Do not forget the one who loves you far beyond your wildest imaginings. Open your arms as wide as you can and visualize double, *triple*, **quadruple**, and **MORE;** that is how much God loves you. God will give you the strength to face anything. His Word says, ✝ *"I can do all things through Him who gives me strength."*

There are so many times in my life I forget God is always with me through thick-or-thin. I know in my head that everything God says is true, but it is not a heart realization. How about you? The problem with the head knowledge of God is that nothing will truly be accomplished in my life. My heart is finally pushing for me to have the right relationship with God, and I'm ready. What got me excited was that I can ask God directly some of my questions and He answers back…talk about the best connection ever! I no longer feel alone, I have the direct channel to Him.

You need strength? He will give it to you. You need a shield from the negative arrows being shot at you? He will put up the shield. You need help with your dreams and goals? He will give you the ability and excitement to move forward. Your only responsibility is to be willing with your heart to thank and praise Him. Don't you think He is worth it? I do with all my heart, but do not fake it. Do the real thing. Again, God says, ✝ *"The Lord is my strength and shield. I trust Him with all my heart. He helps me, and my heart is filled with joy. I burst out in songs of thanksgiving."*

Don't be like me where so many times I forget to step behind God's shield. The silly thing is that even though I know the shield is there I stand there like a fool, being pierced to the heart by satan's arrows. Now that my heart is connected to God, I have asked God to remind me to step behind His shield and be safe. You, too, need to not try and be a warrior and take the shots; it is not cowardice to step behind God's shield. Live a strong and safe life with God.

✝ Philippians 4:11 (NIV)
✝ Psalm 28:7 (NLT)

The Wonder of HIM!

Wonder

This morning the sun was shining, my backyard was full of the different colors of foliage, and the green of the grass was poking its way through the dried leaves. My thoughts were, "How beautiful, and thank you, Lord, for who You are." Why do I say this? It amazes me when I hear some people say that God cannot possibly be real. I really do not know where they come up with that. Open your eyes and watch nature all around you. Everything you see proves who God is and what He wants for you. Remember, He loves you and me unconditionally, and this is His promise to you. You can never do anything that would have Him turn away from you. When I see all nature around me and its perfect order, this is proof to me that God is real. ✝ *"For since the creation of the world God's invisible qualities—His eternal power and divine nature—have been clearly seen, being understood from what has been made, so that men are without excuse."*

The other proof for me are the beautiful sunsets and especially the ocean. How could anyone ever doubt that God is who He says He is? No sunset is ever the same, and no ocean wave comes into the beach the same way, yet everything works in perfect harmony. When I hurt even to my very soul, the ocean is where I will find healing. I have spent hours on the beach under those beautiful sunsets just communing with the Father, Jesus, and the Holy Spirit. What better place than to sit in their presence and just talk with them! It is a wonder and it fills me with such joy. God's unchangeable Word says, ✞*"Those who live at the end of the earth stand in awe of Your wonders. From where the sun rises to where it sets, You inspire shouts of joy."*

Dear friends, be in awe every moment of every day for who God is. You can count on His unconditional love. Raise your hands up *high* in the air to God, and accept His love and all the blessings He has for you.

✞ Romans 1:20 (NIV)
✞ Psalm 65:8 (NLT)

Phew! That's A Relief

Live Moment by Moment

The world is moving at a super nova speed all day long and it seems to never end. How do you keep up with the mad house that is called "your life?" Think about a very busy factory with all the hustle, bustle, and noise that happens when all the factory workers are there. To the untrained person it could become overwhelming. That may be how others see you and maybe see their own lives. This is not normal, even though it may seem so for you. For the sake of your own health and sanity you need a down time to be refreshed. Just sleeping at night will not complete the process...you need to take care of yourself. I don't believe God made you and I to be on constant RUN MODE.

I, personally, am a list maker, to help get the thoughts out of my head so I can move on to the next task at hand. The only problem with my lists was they got so long and involved...I WAS DEPRESSED. The reason for the depression was I knew I would never accomplish anything that was on the list. How do you handle the multitude of duties in your life? When it came to my lists, I tried different ways, such as: write everything down, write everything down but in categories, putting duties on the calendar and highlight in different colors for specific tasks and jobs. You end up with a very colorful calendar and to my eye it looked a mess which didn't help to organize my thoughts. It made it even more cluttered in my mind. I even tried putting the different tasks on post-a-notes and sticking them to my desk. At least, I thought, as I finished a task I could see myself removing the note and throwing it away because at least one item was done. Did any of this make me more efficient or give me the feeling of getting something done? NO. With my lists, notes, categories, and even sticky notes, I was still a frustrated, overwhelmed, and over worked wife, mother, and business owner. Understand that the lists did not cover even the everyday duties of living. My life was a long assembly line that kept **going** and **going** and **going** without any end in sight.

I had one very unpractical solution to my problem…if I stayed up for 24 hours a day for 4 weeks maybe I could get a few things finally off my list. Talk about an impractical and unhealthy way of dealing with your life. That thought flew out of my head as quickly as it had popped in.

We all have a false idea that whatever we cannot complete today we can deal with tomorrow…yeah right! For some reason I had this idea that I was indispensable, like at my job. I remember when my husband would be sick. He felt like if he did not go to work, the company would not be able to function without him. I know in tough times or not you need to always do your best, because there will always be someone else out there willing to do the job. God wants you to take care of yourself. He made you to work to the best of your abilities but He also told you there is a time for rest. God's Word says, ✝"*God my shepherd! I don't need a thing. You have bedded me down in lush meadows, you find me quiet pools to drink from. True to Your word, You let me catch my breath and send me in the right direction. Even when the way goes through Death Valley, I'm not afraid when You walk at my side. Your trusty shepherd's crook makes me feel secure. You serve me a six-course dinner right in front of my enemies. You revive my drooping head; my cup brims with blessings. Your beauty and love chase after me every day of my life. I'm back home in the house of God for the rest of my life.*"

Now it's that time of the day for that blessed rest and renewal of your body and spirit. You already know that when you awaken the next morning, your energy will be renewed and you will be ready for the new day. I want you to consider something that could be a reality for you...THE NEXT MORNING NEVER COMES! My father was one such man! He was told in his forties that he would not live long because of a lung disease. He had surgery to remove the disease but the doctors were unable to remove all of the infected tissue. He was told that one day he would feel a sharp pain and it would be over. I remember growing up with the thought that I may not see my beloved father the next day. Can you even imagine growing up with that constant unknown? That was my life. I never let a moment go by that I did not tell him how much I loved him, especially before I went to bed *every* night.

Dad was always thankful when he woke the next morning. He would say, "Thank you God for giving me another chance to influence others towards You." This, and that special time at night became a tradition and he and I loved; that **daily 'one special moment' together.** I remember my mother told me months after I was married, the first night my father wandered around the house looking for me. You have to realize our tradition had been going on since I was 8 years old. Even though I was married, anytime my parents came for a visit, Dad and I went back to our tradition. I would tiptoe into his room, even though he may be asleep and give him a hug, kiss, and tell him I loved him. When it comes my time to join my family in heaven I will still be tiptoeing up to him to tell him how much I love him. I cannot wait for that joyous reunion and the chance to see him again, but this time when I see him, he will be that healthy, young, vibrant man I never had the privilege of knowing: my father, Adolph Syvert Odegaard.

I was considering something not long ago, about my many lists or attempts at staying organized, and started thinking about what would God want me to do? About that same time I heard a discussion about doing "God's List" instead of mine. I wondered if that could really work and what about everything I had to do? Could I actually get things done on my list? Or was God's list going to consist mainly of studying His Word, prayer, and witnessing? This was something to ponder and ask God what He would have me do. It could not be any worse than what I was doing, because I was getting nowhere fast. Why not try God's List?!

I will tell you the biggest relief for me is knowing that I am doing God's list. Now the pressure is off because I know He will help me get it done...it is awesome. With His list, I always accomplish what I am supposed to do, and feel blessed with the completion of the tasks. When days do not work and everything goes really wrong is when, once again, I try and do it my way. Every time my thinking goes that way...I mess it up. You would think by now I would have learned my lesson, but I guess not, because I have to revisit it many times. Try God's way and see how you feel about it...I love it and I am more willing to even get into the jobs I do not like doing because I know God will be there to help me.

There is a very important step to doing God's List...you need to be listening to Him moment-by-moment. Remember that your past is done...there is nothing you can do about that. The future is unknown...you can have goals and visions but the future has not been written yet. You only have this one moment in time. Doesn't moment-by-moment sound a lot less stressful? Asking God for His direction every moment of every day is what I want for the rest of my life. It is like having a constant conversation with a dear and trusted friend. It is a wonderful feeling.

Here is another realization...God's moment is the medicine for a lousy day...doesn't that sound refreshing? I want God to take control of my day. I know He can do it and I am willing to trust that He knows what is best for me and will protect me from any wrong doings. You may be thinking that God really does not get involved with every aspect of your life. Yes, He does, and I have seen it over and over again. It is not a co-incidence...it is the real deal. Your faith needs to tell you what is God and what is not. Remember the enemy, satan knows the Scriptures as well as God and is always trying to get you to turn away from God's leading. Stay strong in your faith and know that God is who He says He is and you can count on it. The Word says, ✝*"For since the creation of the world God's invisible qualities—His eternal power and divine nature—have been clearly seen, being understood from what has been made, so that men are without excuse."*

My last thought on this subject is what a wonderful God we have that can create the wonders in your life. Don't you want that? Living a moment-by-moment life with God will leave you in awe and wonder at how He can help you with the simplest thing. Did you know that God is a God of detail and that He guarantees to help us? God's Word says, ✝*"Take the old prophets as your mentors. They put up with nothing, went through everything, and never once quit, all the time honoring God. What a gift life is to those who stay the course! You've heard, or course of Job's staying power, and you know how God brought it all together for him at the end. That's because God cares, cares right down to the last detail!"*

When I am at the ocean shores I am reminded of the majesty of God. Every detail is covered from what the ocean's job is to the point of the beauty of the colors and how the waves, sand, wind, everything knows its part of the whole and knows that in completing its part, everything will be to God's design. The results are a beautiful and peaceful ocean scene that will soothe any troubled or jangled spirit. You can experience that peace with God. Instead of being on the super nova train of life, God will give you the time to rest and turn all your worries and moments over to Him. He's waiting for your decision.

What a beautiful life God has planned for you. Not one of fear and anxiety but one of JOY and pleasure as you follow His path.

✝Psalm 23 (The Message)
✝Romans 1:20 (NIV)
✝James 5:11 (The Message)

[27]

God's G.P.S.
Guidance

Your life may feel like a jungle with so many twists and turns, along with the branches and gnarled up roots that trip you with every step you take. Do you feel like you cannot go anywhere without your GPS to guide you? For many of you a GPS is such a necessary part of your daily life. I get lost so easily, even with a GPS I would still get lost or be in an accident because I am watching the box instead of my eyes on the road. My husband and I tease that I would get lost in my own backyard if we had not lived here for so many years. He, on the other hand, has such a sense of direction, that he is his own GPS. I do not know how he does it but he always gets us where we need to go. Here is an example…we were trying to get to a wedding in the Bay Area, we did not even have a map and it was pre-GPS. He kept pointing in an easterly direction and eventually we got there. I remember my dad saying that anyone should be able to follow their nose and get to their destination. My husband did exactly that, and I was so surprised when we pulled up in front of the church…only 5 minutes late.

How do you measure up when you are trying to accomplish something? God is the only *absolute perfect* direction finder. I know that when I get really scrambled and don't seem to know what direction to even go, I call out for God's direction and He comes to my rescue every time. My biggest mistake is when I think I can call on my own abilities to reach my destination. Of course, I miss the road signs and end up on the side of the road in a ditch. I cry out once again to God and He always hears me. That gives me more comfort than any GPS. I have decided since I am not good with any technology, I will call on God's G.P.S. to direct the path for my life.

God's path is not smooth and straight, but when you walk with your hand in His, you WILL NOT fall. His Word says, ✞ *"Show me the right path, O Lord; point out the road for me to follow."* He is there holding you with His strong grip. Know that with God by your side you can do anything. It's your choice. I promise you He is walking with you…just ask. My life has been so much better when I stand strong with God by my side guiding my way.

✞ Psalm 25:4 (NLT)

Lord, I Need a Nap!
Rest

Everything seems to be spiraling out of control and I am exhausted. I need a nap! The only problem is my mind will not let my body rest. Lord, what am I going to do? My "To Do" List at the time was nine pages long, typed, and single-spaced. How was I going to get anything done? The way my body deals with busyness is to shut down instead of working on something. A few weeks earlier, I had finally made a plan for my workload. Pay attention to the phrase *I had finally made a plan*. That should have tipped me off in the first place. Anytime I think I am in control, nothing works out.

Anyway, let me take you back to this new attitude of whittling down the nine pages. I remember doing several things, and I was feeling really good about my accomplishments. It was after lunch and I thought, "Well, I'm going to get back to work." The only problem was fatigue was setting in. Finally, I decided to ask God to help me with the work ahead of me. To my surprise, His answer was my next activity was to <u>rest</u>. I argued with God that I had too much to do that day. My first mistake was I thought I would win the argument...wrong. I knew I needed to follow what God said but I was worried. You see in my past, when I would take a nap I was out for 2 hours. I did not have that kind of time to waste. This was another experience when I followed His direction and to my surprise, I rested for 30 minutes and was up totally and completely refreshed. I accomplished more than I would have ever done if I had pushed through. The amazing thing was that I had energy left over and I completed more work than expected.

When I let God into my day it goes so much smoother. I have also realized, when God says "rest" I will no longer argue with Him. He knows what I can do and He will be there. I just have to remember to ask Him for every choice I make and not let satan distract me from God's voice. His Word says, ✞ *"Come to me, all of you who are weary and carry heavy burdens, and I will give you rest."*

I know with all my heart that I never have to walk or carry a burden alone. Sometimes it can be so heavy that if God was not there I would be crushed from the weight of it. Give it over to Him, even if it is just time to take a nap. My life is so much easier when I ask God what to do. I now ask God to help me say no to *self and* <u>YES</u> to what God wants in every moment of my life. When God is involved with your day it is like someone carrying the groceries to the car for you. The help He gives is so much grander than any bag of groceries. Your soul can truly rest with God.

✞ Matthew 11:28 (NLT)

Sunsets In My Life
Special & Unique

In times of reflection, you want to see the beauty of your life. There may be times you think there is nothing special about you. I want you to put your name in this verse: ✝ "**Your name**, *You are fearfully and wonderfully made.*" Do you think that God would have taken the time to tell you this in His Word if you are not special and unique in His eyes? Your life is as unique as any sunsets that can be seen all over the world. That represents more sunsets than our mind can even comprehend. It boggles the mind...the blessing is you do not have to remember them. You just have to remember that you are unique and special.

Let's take this little trip into the realm of sunsets. I am sure you have seen many sunsets that were amazing and unique. I have seen some that took my breath away. Many know all about how the sunsets are created and all the technical reasons, but do not think about that today. I want you to think about the beauty and what inspiration you get by watching them, as the sun slowly goes down behind the horizon. When my husband and I were on our cruises, I loved watching the sunset every night. They were magnificent and each uniquely different in themselves.

What was the mystery as each one painted its own glorious picture in the sky? Only God knows and my inner spirit. But I knew without a doubt that God was speaking to my heart. He knows what He is saying to me and I just trust Him knowing that He cares and watches over me. My husband and I were amazed as we watched the many sunsets which ranged from being in a clear sky to the stormy sky of a hurricane. Each one was unique and had a special meaning for that day. What I wouldn't give to see those awesome sunsets once again!

Many times I have been in a situation when, of course, I did not have my camera to capture the sight before me. But the memory of each one stays with me. In my disappointment, I remind myself that there will be others that can inspire me to greatness and beauty within my own life. You may be thinking, "It is just a sunset to watch, how can it be an inspiration in your life?" When I watch these sunsets, I am quiet and in awe of it...many times this is when God speaks to me. Maybe I have been confused and clarity comes; the feeling of sadness and this will lift my spirit; or if everything is well in my life, then it reminds me of the wonderful changes God has made in my life. He even shows me visions in those beautiful rays.

On the other hand, just like not having the camera to capture the vision, it saddens me to realize the opportunities that God has waiting for me, that I missed. Have you been aware of such opportunities? You need to be aware of the "now" in your life. When you follow God's "now" it will help you get to what He really wants for you. Isn't that a glorious thought that you can hold onto when times get rough? God is your lighthouse through those storms and the sunsets are His reminders that He has once again been there for you. I believe it...do you?

Let's talk about relating your life to the stages of a beautiful sunset. Let me first set the scene of these awesome sunsets. It was December 2009 at Clear Lake, California. We stood on the shore of the lake watching how the simple sunset changed into these waves of colors. Who would have thought that simple act of the sun dropping behind the horizon would paint such a glorious wave of richness and colors in the sky.

When you live in the big city, flat land with trees and buildings blocking every site, like I did, it is difficult to watch the sunsets. When I was a child we lived on a hill high above the city and the bright lights. I would go out on my front porch and watch the sunsets whenever I could. What a glorious sight for a young, impressionable mind. When I think of the obstacles that were in my way to stop me from watching God's wonders, I would become angry. I wanted to see His miraculous sunsets. This was a perfect example of looking at the bad side of my life and especially becoming angry about it. Instead, I needed to remind myself of the awesome sunsets I have seen. It is so easy to let myself dwell on what I did not get to do, instead of what I GOT TO DO especially with God's help.

Here's a possible day...It starts with your first thoughts upon waking in the morning. This is the beginning of your sunset. Are your thoughts on the one who can truly guide the resolution of your sunset throughout the day? Or when you wake up in the morning, you think, "Oh, I have to deal with that nasty situation that didn't get resolved yesterday...**oh poor me**. It's going to ruin my whole day." Think about the way you want your sunset to develop. If you continue the pattern you started with, it will never develop into that beautiful sunset God wants for you...it will be ordinary and dull. Wouldn't you rather it be unbelievable? In any situation you could get trapped into having a bad attitude. Instead you should look at it as an opportunity to let God show you, once again, that He cares for you.

I want to side-step a little here. Your daily life can be affected by the way you think about yourself. God looks at you this way, ✝"...*rejected by men but chosen by God and precious to Him.*" I want you to think about what makes you special and unique. There is only one of you. God made you special and you really need to believe this. If you do not...STOP and thank God for why He made you the way you are. This is a good thing. **Remember, YOU ARE**

PRECIOUS TO HIM. Now let us get back to your sunset day.

When situations arise…this is the beginning of your sunset. What are you seeing as it progresses? Are you focusing on the bad stuff or do you see the hand of God helping you to move to the next rays and colors of your sunset? Many of you can be so quick to look at only the bad things that are happening, not realizing that when you turn your eyes to God, He will make something beautiful. Which result do you want? Remember what His Word says, ✝*"Take the old prophets as your mentors. They put up with anything, went through everything, and never once quit, all the time honoring God. What a gift, life is to those who stay the course! You have heard, of course, of Job's staying power, and you know how God brought it all together for him at the end. That's because God cares, cares right down to the last detail."*

One thing I have learned is that with God every moment can be beautiful; you just need to want it. To change your life or situation is to just pray. <u>God is a prayer-answering God</u> (I believe). This is what comes to my mind when I see a sunset, because I know God is answering the prayers I have not even uttered yet.

Say it again … <u>God is a prayer-answering God</u> (I believe)

Are you beginning to believe what you are saying? Do you understand that He can change every situation in your life and make a beautiful sunset out of each day? Say this sentence again, but with passion and conviction.

God is a prayer-answering God

(I believe & I will receive)

Think about your day…did it close with the completion of a beautiful sunset or did it seem to go from one simple beautiful sunset to black with no beauty at all. WHAT WAS YOUR DAY LIKE? When you stay focused on God your sunsets will progress from its simple beauty to its magnificent ending.

I have been out on the beach or someplace lovely and once again, an amazing sunset…of course NO CAMERA. The tendency is to be frustrated and beat yourself up that you did not plan ahead and had your camera to catch the sight. How many times do you do that in your everyday life? Again this is a time when instead of living in the frustration and anger, turn it over to God. Release the pain of missing something, and take the picture with the camera in your heart. God will help you deal with it. It can be very easy to say this. You might be thinking, "If she really knew what I was dealing with, she wouldn't say that." Believe me, I do know the feeling and I'm here to say…TURN IT OVER TO GOD. He is there waiting for you to come to His arms and He will give you the strength to take the next step.

Walk hand and hand with Him…you won't regret it.

Each day of your life can be a sunset of richness and beauty. If someone was looking at the sunset in your life, what would their reaction be? Would their reactions be, "That sunset was okay, but I have seen better in other people's lives." Or would the comments be, "WOW, what an unbelievable sunset!" God wants us to have a life full of WOW moments and He is the one that will help us get there.

You would agree with me that there are never two sunsets that are the same. You would also agree with me that there are no two **(Your name)** that are the same. Can you make a change as the new day approaches? The dawn comes with yet another beautiful sunrise! Focus your attention on what God has for you today. God is so wonderful that He sees the uniqueness of each of you. He will make your life more beautiful than the sunsets. Can you really take in what this means in your life? You know the saying…"you are looking at life through rose colored glasses." It is time to look at your life through "God's colored glasses" and see the wonder He has in store for you…RIGHT NOW! Follow His steps and be freed from a life of fear, and live your life in JOY.

✝Psalm 139:14 (New King James)
✝1 Peter 2:4 (NIV)
✝James 5:11 (The Message)

My Mess in Life
All of Me

I want you to really think on what God says here: ✝"*So here's what I want you to do, God helping you: Take your everyday, ordinary life—your sleeping, eating, going-to-work, and walking-around life—and place it before God as an offering. Embracing what God does for you is the best thing you can do for Him. Don't become so well-adjusted to your culture that you fit into it without even thinking. Instead, fix your attention on God. You'll be changed from the inside out. Readily recognize what He wants from you, and quickly respond to it. Unlike the culture around you, always dragging you down to its level of immaturity, God brings the best out of you, develops well-formed maturity in you.*"

Many of us know Romans 12:1-2 but when I read it in The Message it really hit home. I realize that anything of this earth is nothing without God. Looking at this phrase, *"everyday, ordinary life..."* God is saying to me, that He wants to be involved in every part of my life. I do not need to depend on others to show me the way. God is interested in the smallest part of my life...THAT MEANS ALL OF ME! It is so easy to get caught up in everything around you. This life is okay but I do not need to accept what the influences of this world tell me is right. Daily influences can be extremely negative and can pull me down. Instead, I want what God wants for me, and I am ready for whatever it takes to be mature in God.

The other statement to focus on is that I am to *"fix MY attention on God."* This reminds me...the earth is my temporary home. I know with certainty that I am God's daughter and I need to focus my attention on Him. I cannot wait until it is my turn to go home to be with my Heavenly Father. How about you? To finally understand all the questions I have here on earth will be revealed to me. To not have to worry about my next paycheck, where I am going to live, what I am going to eat, or if I am going to wake up with that painful body once again.

All I have to do is *"recognize what He wants from ME, and quickly respond to it."* I say what joy to be forever with God. Dear reader...you should be jumping with joy as you prayerfully absorb every bit of what this verse is saying to your heart. Take in all the blessings and be thankful. I am; you should be too!

✝ Romans 12:1-2 (the Message)

Help Me, Jesus!
Help

You can be so wrapped up in the BUSYNESS of life that you see nothing good; just possible disaster. Did you realize that being that busy is satan's way of getting your focus off of God and onto your*self*? This is no way to live your life. It will wear you out physically, emotionally, and even spiritually. When your life is topsy-turvy, do you ever stop and think, "I wonder who could help me?" The answer is Jesus. Did you realize all you have to do is say, "Help me Jesus," and He will be there for you? What an amazing comfort in everything and I mean *everything, that you put your hand and mind to.*

When these feelings come, you need to be praying for His guidance and expect His peace. If you have never experienced the peace of God, try it! You will like it. Right now, my world is up in the air and so many things are on my plate that my head hurts just to think about it. At the end of the day it seems like I don't get anything done. I am constantly being pulled in multiple directions. Do I always think of God first to help? Not always, and my head hurts even more. I know He is there without a doubt. As usual, I let satan in and he creates the next trap to make my life go

[43]

crazy once again. Look at what God has to say, ✟ *"Now may the Lord of Peace Himself give you peace at all times and in every way. The Lord be with you."* I can tell you from experience that when I accept Jesus' peace it is like a breath of fresh air. What a beautiful experience! No need to worry anymore. My response is, "Thank you, Jesus, for once again being my rescuer." Remember that you can call out to Jesus every moment of every day if you need Him. He is never too busy for you.

My prayer for you is, "Father, God, give peace to the reader and help them to look to you in times of feeling out of control with the busyness of life." Let the reader be willing to cry out, "Jesus, help me that I might know you are there." Amen

✟ 2 Thessalonians 3:36 (NIV)

From Darkness to Light
Fear & Depression

My husband and I were on a cruise in the North Atlantic Ocean heading towards Iceland. I was sitting in my cabin looking out into the dark and the blackness of the sea. I felt the gloom and foreboding wash over my spirit as I sat there. I could not believe my eyes when in the far distance a very small spot of light appeared, as if by magic. As the minutes slowly went by the light grew larger. As we approached, I realized it was a lighthouse with its light stretching out into the horizon giving comfort and direction. The spring of hope once again lifted my spirit and I knew each step on this unknown journey would have the loving guidance from this tower of strength. Just from my own feelings of exhilaration I can only image the relief this towering beacon gives to ships and weary travelers searching for rest.

How many times do you spend thinking about all your fears or the troubles in your life? You just want someone to give you the guidance to save you from that feeling of ultimate doom. The fear is like looking out into the black night with not even a star in the sky. It reminds you of days when it seems like there is no hope and all you see is doom and gloom. Do you realize the devastation that the negative thinking will do to you spiritually, physically, and emotionally? What is your spirit to do when that happens? I feel sorry for those who have no hope and despair to the point of possible suicide. How sad it is to get to the point in your life that the only road you see is death. But death can come in many forms. It might be suicide because you just cannot face life anymore or it may be death of the spirit. Either way you are willing to end something precious that God has created. You are sinning against Him when you even have the thought of ending what He created. How dare you even think such a thing! Instead look at the "JOY" in your life. Your first thought may be, "That's the point! There is no joy in my life. All I know is fear and worry." Throughout God's Word you will find scriptures you can meditate on to encourage you even at your darkest moment.

I sit here at night looking out at the blackness of the ocean and not being able to see the waves or anything of God's glory in the ocean blue. I have a sense of being separated from Him, which means no loving arms to run to or be comforted in—totally alone in this massive world. Me, feeling so small and insignificant, how could I cope with life itself? This terrifies me! What would the world truly be like with no God to come to your rescue, or be there to comfort you?

A parallel story about darkness and the desire for someone to save you is when I was living in Oregon with my husband, Rick and we went out with friends of ours for the day. When we were driving home after having a wonderful day it was pitch dark. We decided to stop at a rest stop off Interstate 5. While my friend and I were in the restroom freshening up, our husbands decided to walk down the path to the river. I knew from a previous experience that there were trees running down the path to the river. I did not remember how far it was but my friend and I decided to walk that path.

As we were walking down, I became more and more anxious, and the fear of someone jumping out and attacking us overwhelmed me. At that time there had been reports of a violent criminal, called the I-5 Rapist that was travelling up and down the freeway. I had always been afraid of being at the mercy of someone that I could not defend myself against. This was the thought running wild in my mind as we walked that path to the river. I felt like it would never end. I became more and more agitated until I was screaming for Rick. When we finally found each other I was screaming and frantically pounding on his chest about how dare he leave me alone. With his calm demeanor he held me and just let me fall apart. Then, with his reassuring arms and voice questioned me, "Babe, why are you so angry and scared? Once I told him, he said, "Don't you know by now, that I will never leave you?" At that moment, I was reassured of the love and comfort I could always count on. This calmed my heart and I was now at peace in my heart and soul.

This story also reminded me of the times when I was so afraid in my life, but when I looked God was there to hold me and carry me through the danger. This also is a perfect example of the poem "Footprints." If you have not read it, I suggest you do. What a perfect example when you keep God in your life He promises to be there even when you only see one set of footprints in the sand. Do you ever feel like you were alone? Or were you not looking and realizing that God is carrying you through the trials in your life. What a wonderful assurance to know that God will always be there with you no matter what.

Take a moment right now and think about the "fear" that is gripping you and maybe you feel like there is a strangle hold on you. Now you are at the point where you cannot breathe, or any step you try to make is being blocked. Every time you try and move forward you feel like you are being dragged back even further into that fear. What can you do? Do you believe that God is strong enough to pull you out of your desperation? Is He a big enough God for you? He can help you conquer this fear, whether it is spiritual, physical, or even emotional. Your action should be, "I'm running as fast as I can to the only one that is my haven of rest—the arms of God. This is the time that doubt, who is actually satan, will raise his ugly head to tell you that you cannot possibly believe that. God knows everything, so wouldn't He be your source in times of trouble?

I remember when my husband and I were at the end of our ropes in a legal battle over our first home and it looked like we were going to lose everything. I was so terrified with the fact that everything we had worked for would be gone. I cried and cried, and had the "oh woe is me," blues until I could not even function. The thoughts that hounded me were, "This is our first home, and they have cheated us out of our dream." Of course, this made me angrier and the thoughts once again of, "How dare they do this to us!" We were talking with the attorney on what we would be facing, and blackness awaited us at every turn. My once again, calm husband looked at the attorney and said, "I have a job and I can still put a roof over our heads, and food on the table. What more do we need than that." Rick was right and to God's glory and grace we actually came out of the real estate fraud better than ever expected. We went from owning a townhouse to our own beautiful home on a quarter acre of land in beautiful Corvallis, Oregon. God supplied more than what we had originally had and it was more of a family home that our future son would share with us a few years later. This was another one of those situations that could have been a disaster but in the end we turned our eyes to God and He was there as promised.

When you think about God's love and know that He wants the best for you, this is what you need to do. Remember the days when you were small and you could run to the loving arms of your father, or some other strong and loving role model in your life, and know you were safe and secure? That is the vision of God — with arms opened wide waiting for you to run to Him with all speed and FEEL those warm loving arms around you. What a comfort, just knowing that He is too big for any harm to fall upon you, as long as you stay in that warm embrace.

When it is time to venture out go with His assurance that He will give you the strength to face what is in front of you. Face that ordeal with renewed strength and direction. Here is a scripture you can count on, ✝ *"But those who hope in the Lord will renew their strength. They will soar on wings like eagles; they will run and not grow weary, they will walk and not be faint."* What a great assurance, at times of overwhelmed and the feeling of impending disaster. He promises to renew your strength and then you can take the next step, no matter how small.

✝*"May the God of hope fill you with all joy and peace as you trust in Him, so that you may overflow with hope by the power of the Holy Spirit."* Remember this when you count on God through any circumstance, it is like taking a check to the bank. Your account will grow. Is God's "check" good? — you can bank on it!

When you are out in the ocean and there is nothing but blackness then shines that glorious beacon of light from the lighthouse to lead the way home. Be thankful and joyous for that simple act lighting the way. In your life God is that grand lighthouse that will guide you through the turmoil and the troubled waters to a calm and glorious new day where the sun rises once more.

Do you have that life gripping fear that terrifies you to the point of no return? Identify your fear and give it to God to carry that burden for you. He can set you free! Set your mind and heart to say, "NEVER AGAIN will I focus on fear but know that ✝*"God has not given me a spirit of fear, but one of power, love, and a sound mind."* Allow God to fill you with His everlasting love. God can take away that fear if you will let Him. Now take your next step and give Him all the glory.

The bottom line is this…to find hope and rest in times of trouble you need to have a relationship with God. He will always be there for you in your deepest despair. Have the assurance that you can count on Him every day. God is your strength and He promises to help you through your circumstances and you can take God's check to the bank.

✝Isaiah 40:31 (NIV)
✝Romans 15:13 (NIV)
✝2 Timothy 1:7 (New Kings James)

Miracles Happen
Miracles

    In the Bible there are many examples of Jesus Christ and His miracles. My question is...do you believe in miracles? It does not seem that in this modern day miracles are observed like in Christ's time. But think about it; they didn't have all the *stuff* we have today. The Word says, ✝*"Then Jesus said to him, unless you see signs and miracles happen, you [people] never will believe (trust, have faith) at all."* I personally believe that miracles happen all the time; we are just *sooo* busy with life and all the noise from our technology blocks what God is showing us.

    There are those that talk about meditation. For me it is just slowing down my busyness so I can watch and listen for the miracles of God. I grew up with a Father that was very ill. We did not know when he would take his last breath and I would be without a father. I knew that his days were numbered, even when I was only five years old. My whole life with him was one big question mark. My father passed in 1992 and was 73 years old. He was not expected to live long enough to see his two kids grow up, or to even reach his forties. I never knew when I woke up if Dad would still be here. Every night before I went to bed, I always found him on his bed and would go in and say, "I love you, Dad." I wanted to make sure that he knew that. The next morning to the joy of my young heart, he would be there and I was so thankful that I would have him for one more day.

Even the smallest things like when I am in traffic and I get to my destination safe and sound, talking with a friend, praying for someone's needs and then seeing the answers to those prayers...these are all miracles. The miracle of having a roof over my head, food to eat, a life with meaning and purpose is so real. These are just a few, but the point is that miracles do happen...just look and listen. Miracles are God's proof that He cares about me and I love Him for the reminder of who He is.

As the verse says, God's miracles are to give my weak mind something to hold onto so that I do not forget what God has done for me. Make a list of the miracles that you have seen. I believe in them and as I watch for them, I thank God for them.

✝ John 4:48 (AMP)

Satan Loves a Clutter Queen

Discombobulated

There are times that you do not know why all the plans you had all of a sudden get all *discombobulated*. You are confused because you had a plan of action...everything that you are told you need to accomplish your goals. I know for me this state of mind is because the evil doer is hard at work once again. God's Word says, ✝ *"You were running superbly! Who cut in on you, deflecting you from the true course of obedience? This detour doesn't come from the One who called you into the race in the first place. And please don't toss this off as insignificant. It only takes a minute amount of yeast, you know, to permeate an entire loaf of bread. Deep down, the Master has given me confidence that you will not deflect. But the one who is upsetting you, whoever he is, will bear the divine judgment."*

I believe that satan uses clutter, confusion, and disorganization to stop us from paying attention to what God wants. For me, as I see piles of clutter on my desk, I start feeling guilty because I am not staying on top of stuff. Satan tries to convince me that God's way is not fun. When I think about it, life is so much better with God rather than with satan. This is one of satan's lies...remember he is the ultimate liar. So how do I stop him? I just need to remember to stay focused on **God** and not satan's lies.

So many times I am weak and can't seem to stay on track. That is when I need to get back into the scriptures. If there is not time for that, I just ask God to get me back on track. For most of my life I was never taught to have a really personal, one-on-one relationship with God. Praying once a day was fine, but I knew nothing about the moment-by-moment living with God and what a joy it is. This has been such a change in my thinking that satan keeps attacking me saying that my previous relationship with God was just fine, so why change it? Now that I am having a two-way conversation with God, I want more, and satan is fighting back as hard as he can to stop me.

My first step in making this change is to start my day in His Word to fill my mind with Him. Then it's to ask God for His help in everything I do every day. It sounds easy, right? It isn't, because satan is always trying to block God's voice. Each day I wake up asking God to fill my mind. My moment-by-moment prayer is to keep my mind focused and not *discombobulated* with clutter. If there needs to be clutter, let it be cluttered with God.

✝ Galatians 5:7-10 (The Message)

Fjords of Your Life vs. Majesty

God vs. Me

In my dreams, last night, I saw massive cliffs before me; I stood there in awe of the majesty and grandeur. I am struck by how insignificant and small I am by comparison. The cliffs stand straight and tall, full of life, strength, and protection. My life looms before me, bent, weak, and vulnerable. Could there be a plan for my life? Am I on the right path spiritually to grow like these massive fjords with God?

In 2005, my husband and I were on a cruise ship, sailing in the North Atlantic. We went to some wonderful places but there is one I will never forget. On our way to Greenland, we went through Prince Christian Sound. We saw the beautiful fjords, snow peaks, and even the icebergs. This was a place that many ships could not go because of the dangers lying at every turn.

In all this massiveness of these large mountains stood this quaint village on what looked like a small lip of the cliff. It looked as though this small village was isolated from the whole world and probably forgotten. What would it be like to be so out of touch with everything around you? We, along with the other passengers pondered as the ship went by. One observation I saw was that their homes were so colorful in this small village. I found out later that the homes were colorful on purpose so that when there was a snow storm the houses could easily be seen. The hardships, living there, had to be very difficult, so why go there? It seems like the people living there were crazy, knowing that to live in that environment would be hard...but there they were in all their colorful glory.

There have been many cliffs in my life, but I let them defeat me and allow me to give up. How foolish is that? I have since learned that I need to be thankful for the blessings that will come from the "challenge" that God is presenting me. Satan is going to attack me from every angle but once I set myself firm in God's Word, I can be like the fjords.

God's Word says, ✝*"Embrace this God-life. Really embrace it, and nothing will be too much for you. This mountain, for instance: Just say, 'Go jump in the lake'—no shuffling or shilly-shallying—and it's as good as done. That's why I urge you to pray for absolutely everything, ranging from small to large. Include everything as you embrace this God-life, and you'll get God's everything."*

I relate the majesty of the fjords to our great God. Is He big enough for you? When you can trust that God is there for you no matter what, you have no reason to fear. God will help you achieve the success He wants for you. When you fear is when the enemy attacks. It is not a frontal attack, because you can see it coming. The attack, from the enemy, is through deception and confusion. In this the enemy (satan) uses fear to stop you from succeeding. You need to STOP him in his tracks so he can no longer hurt or frighten you. Once again, HOW BIG IS YOUR GOD??!! My God is **huge** and He can do anything and will protect me from the flaming arrows that satan flings at me. If your God is not huge, then this will leave room for the enemy (deceiver) to trap you and get you off track. Like the cliff vs. the village, compare your abilities to God's. How do you measure up?

Your obstacles could be small or huge but they can be damaging to the point of death...emotionally and spiritually. The situation may seem small to begin with, but like the icebergs, you are only seeing the tip of the situation. The most dangerous part is looming below the surface to destroy you. It can be without any warning. You don't want to get too close without some awareness and protection of what is below. God's Word is that source...measure your actions up to God's standards. When decisions and relationships are being made, your spiritual rudder will steer you into safe harbor. If you trust Him, God will guide you but the KEY is *trust* Him and believe His Word. Even during times of trouble God is walking right alongside, helping all the way. He promises He will not let go of you and He is a God of details. God is a PRAYER-answering God. In His Word it says, ✝ *"Nothing is too hard!"*

While on our journey together, let's go back to that tiny village on the cliff. As we passed that small village there was an unexpected surprise. Behind this massive mountain there was a channel of water flowing behind that mountain. It would have been interesting to explore closer to see exactly where it went. My guess was that it was probably the way in and out of that small village. God is so great to find a way to give you what you need, even in the roughest times in your life, like this small village. Doesn't this just amaze you how God, without any warning will surprise you and everything seems to work together? I love the fact that God is working out all the details. Why worry? God is on the job!

The end of the journey is to acknowledge *once and for all* God in your life. He is the master controller and willing, if asked, to lead you through your life. He knows your future and will reveal it as you need to know. I realize that sometimes this is frustrating because we want to see it all right now, not get it in pieces. What are you worrying about? Again, do you trust Him to have your best interest at heart?

I would much rather that He is in control than me. I don't know about you, but I would make a mess of my life and then wonder why it happened. This is a majestic God that has your best interest at heart. Plus, the miracle is that He works with everyone that you come in contact with and He knows their heart and can mesh your lives together. By doing so, He will help everyone succeed and have a better quality of life.

Are you ready for it? I am…come join me on another journey, but this time it will be a threesome and God will be with us. His Word says, ✝ *"Two are better than one, because they have a good return for their work: If one falls down, his friend can help him up. But pity the man who falls and has no one to help him up! Also, if two lie down together, they will keep warm. But how can one keep warm alone? Though one may be overpowered, two can defend themselves. A cord of three strands is not quickly broken."* Make God your third strand and you will be unshakable…like the quaint village on the lip of the majestic cliffs, that village is unmovable because of the solid foundation. God is your foundation and you can count on it.

✝Mark 11:22-24 (The Message)
✝Jeremiah 32:17 (The Message)
✝Ecclesiastes 4:9-12 (NIV)

Effortless Running River

Dreams

In the beautiful city of Fort Lauderdale, Florida, ran the river of what I would like to call "gold." On either side of the river were the most beautiful homes, many with a history of their own. There it felt like you were in yacht alley, not just little boats but enormous ships that looked like floating hotels. During the ride down the river, we learned from our guide about the owners. I was amazed that one small family or a couple would own something so massive. The meandering of the river through this valley of gold gave me a moment to pause and reflect on my overwhelming emotions. The sight that stood before me took my breath away, and gave me that feeling of amazement. At the same time slowly floating down this city river gave me a sense of calm and wonder. My thoughts would turn to, "Who are these people that live in such luxury, whether a mansion, yacht, or maybe both?" Still all around these golden wonders life continued on as if nothing was out of the ordinary or different from the rest of the world. Upon our return, the thrill of a river, literally full of lights everywhere blew me away. Talk about an amazing sight! Seeing all the glory and once again, it brought me to a point to pause and wonder...

[63]

What is the difference between you, me, and the people that live at the 'river of gold?' It is the simple fact of dreaming and then working the dream. Dreams can come in different forms. It is not always to be wealthy and have no cares at all. Your dreams, as mine, might be totally different or they may be the same. I base my dreams on what God wants for my life. It is easy to say, "Whatever you want for me Lord" and then go on your merry little way ignoring the steps God has planned for you. The first step is to write your dream in detail. This turns the thoughts into something tangible that can be worked on. It also makes it a reality that WILL HAPPEN.

I will never forget an incident in 2006. As an inspirational speaker, I wanted to put on my own Women's Retreat. I already had the vision of the name, "Renewing Your Spirit." The one fear of mine was that it could not be a spiritual retreat because I didn't know enough. Besides that, who would want to come and listen to what I had to say on the subject? In fact, what would the subjects even be about? I wanted to be safe and on the fence and not offend anyone with the event. In general I talked about it so much, I'm sure my family and friends were getting tired of hearing about it. I had the opportunity through an organization I belonged to for two free sessions with a marketing coach. We talked about many things and once again I brought up this idea of a Women's Retreat. She said one thing to me that changed everything: "When & Where?" I was on that phone stumped into total silence. My first thoughts were, "Oh no, what have I gotten myself into? What was I going to do?" I had one more session and she wanted my answer by the next month. I can tell you that entire month, I worried myself almost to the point of being sick.

That whole month I could not make up my mind: there are so many places to go, should it be in the fall, winter, spring, or summer, how long should it be, and how would I ever figure the cost. Understand; I have always had a problem with pricing. It had been drummed into my head to not give away the store. My only problem was, in my insecurity of not having any degrees or background, what gave me the right to give my opinion? The overall question for the month was, "How was I ever going to come up with the answers?" This should not have been hard: remember, it was a dream of mine so what is the big deal? It was not like I was planning a huge conference, maybe 20 women. It became a huge obstacle for me and that old thought of, "who would want to come to something I put on, once again plagued me?!"

When I had my next session, the first question was, "Well?" At this point I still had not made up my mind on anything. I took a deep breath; paused; blew out the little bit of breath still in my lungs and said, "Carmel, the month of April 2007." This was only going to give me 5 months to plan. I thought to myself, "YOU ARE CRAZY!" Once I said it, I knew it would happen and it became a reality. We went to the Carmel Valley Lodge in Carmel Valley and had a marvelous time. Was it perfect? Of course not, but we did have lots of fun. There was still some reserve in my presentations because I was still a little afraid of the ladies getting the wrong idea, so the subjects remained very general. No threat to anyone! I did a second retreat the following year in the Mendocino area but once again, I wanted to be very careful not to offend anyone by having the retreat TOO spiritual.

I love how God will help us address even the silliest of our fears. One month after the retreat to Mendocino I had decided to plan a second one at the same location in 2009. Everyone seemed happy with the retreat, so why not do the same thing for 2009, I thought. WRONG! God had another idea and He would not let me go any other direction. Even though the enemy, satan was doing everything possible to discourage me, it was to be a spiritually based weekend. Talk about fear, but God had promised me that every woman would break barriers that weekend. I was, once again, afraid. I am happy to report, and in total awe of God's magnificent power, by the end of the weekend, every one of those nine women broke through a major barrier in their life. What a great God we have! He even proved Himself more by sending three eagles to fly overhead on the morning of my discouragement about how the retreat was going; maybe the promise was not going to be fulfilled.

Those eagles were the reminder that God was there and the miracle would happen. Thank you Lord, for your steadfastness and answer to your promise to show your strength to my doubting spirit.

Once again, dreams are only as big as you can imagine. God's visions for us are even bigger if we are willing to walk with Him moment-by-moment and follow His direction. On one of our trips, we went through the Panama Canal...now there was a HUGE dream fulfilled. What would have happened if the authors of this project had given up because it just seemed too hard? Their dream of a canal helping the travelers get from one side of the continent to the other without extending the trip tenfold had created this marvelous landmark that helps and amazes millions. Whether your dreams are small or large, God is there to guide you all the way if you are willing.

As you think about the locks, which raises the water level either up or down so the ships can pass, you may have the need to raise the levels of your dream. You want to have a continued connection with God. He is your pipeline to achievement. When you are walking in step with Him you may find some bumps or curves and the path may not be completely straight but we need to be praying, ♱*"I'm single-minded in pursuit of you; don't let me miss the road signs you've posted."* God has blessings and favors waiting for you as you walk this line with Him.

There are things that the enemy uses to stop you and get you off course from your dreams. Some of the biggest stoppers are your emotions like doubt, worry, and one of the biggest of all is the feeling of unworthiness. You know those thoughts like, "I'm not good enough to have my dreams fulfilled." "I don't know enough to accomplish anything." "Why try, I never finish anything I set out to do." How about this one? "I'm not very intelligent and smart enough for anything good to come my way."

I am sure you may have an old story that is running in your head. I want you to be aware of where that old story is coming from. It is the deceiver, satan. First he gets you listening to it, then he gets you to think on it, then he gets you to dwell on it, and then he gets you to act on it. By turning any one of those steps over to God, it will CUT the hold he has over you. Instead of letting the deceiver trap you, surround yourself with the words of encouragement from God. Listen, think, dwell, then ACT on God's Word and direction and your path will be smooth. I didn't say it would be easy, but it will be smoother and you have your pilot in the main seat heading you towards success and fulfillment of your dreams and His vision for your life.

Sometimes, even when you are trying to follow God, it may feel like you are alone but this is where faith comes in and you need to trust that He is there. Do you believe Him? I do! Even in my weakest moments I know He is there ready to guide me along. What do you believe? Are you ready to trust Him?

When things are not working out use this statement:

In times of distress, instead of talking about all the problems…talk about the GOD of POSSIBILITIES!

✝Psalm 119: 10 (The Message)

Beauty of the Lights in the Distance

God's Guiding Light

"Don't panic. I'm with you. There's no need to fear for I'm your God. I'll give you strength. I'll help you. I'll hold you steady, and keep a firm grip on you." --Isaiah 41:10 (The Message)

Are there times when you feel like a small child and you don't know which direction is home? You are lost and all alone. You start thinking about your mommy and daddy...you may be excited or frightened but you are still scared because you have lost your way. Sometimes you may feel like you are climbing a stairway that seems to lead to nowhere. ***Who or what is waiting for you at the top of the stairs...GOOD OR EVIL!*** As a child, I remember at my grandmother's home in Oakland, California the dark narrow stairs going to her basement. They creaked and groaned as you walked down those rickety stairs. I knew I would fall to my death as they seemed to give a little more with each and every step. The stairway was so narrow and it went deeper and deeper into what seemed an endless dark hole. I felt like I was stepping into the depths of hell...I was terrified! On the other hand, if I walked into her living room, there was a beautiful wooden staircase that led up to the upstairs of this beautiful 3 story home. I would find beautifully decorated rooms with the richness and warmth along with the scent of lavender and spice…this was what heaven must be like, surrounded by love. The upstairs was so different from the basement with all its hidden dangers.

In your life, the staircase may be narrow, dark, scary, as you carefully creep up the stairwell. You know there are dangers as you round each corner of this frightening and gloomy place, but there seems no other way to get to your destination. Wouldn't you rather climb a staircase full of that reassuring light with beautiful wood handrails leading you to your future? The stairs are easier and because of the warm and inviting light, the dangers are seen before they can cause devastation. It almost feels like you are being guided by the hand to the life of your dreams and fulfillment. This is the life that God wants for you and He will be your guide through and around the obstacles, so you won't fall or trip. God says, ✝*"By your words I can see where I'm going; they throw a beam of light on my dark path."* God also gives you a promise of guidance through your life. Anything God says can be trusted and then you can rest in His assurance. He says, ✝*"I am the world's light. No one who follows me stumbles around in the darkness. I provide plenty of light to live in."* What a blessing to know that with God and His Son, Jesus Christ, you will be guided throughout your life. But maybe that is not enough assurance for you. If not, why not?

I grew up in the hills of Hayward, California that overlooked the San Francisco Bay Area. You could tell what kind of a day it would be, whether clear, overcast, and even if the smog levels were high. What I loved the most was sitting out on the front lawn and looking over the Bay at night. What a sight with all the beautiful white lights of the city. It was breathtaking to see the outline of the Bay in its blackness against the border of lights surrounding the one side. The blackness made me ponder on what life truly would be like without God. The beautiful lights were like a beacon to some place wonderful and unexpected. I would sit there in wonder about how it must grieve God about those who choose an evil life instead of what He has in store for them. Then my thoughts would pause and think about the majesty, wonder, and beauty of who God is...

My thoughts turn to wondering. If we have the choice of a good world for everyone vs. a world full of evil, which would seem more appealing? I am not saying a little bit of both but one that is truly GOOD and one that is truly EVIL. In the good world you would, without question follow God's direction every moment of every day without any hesitation. In the world of evil God would not be there and you would be at the mercy of every evil act no matter how depraved. You would have to live out your life in that world with absolutely no hope.

There is an answer…you can let God guide your path and be willing, no matter what, to accept His direction for your life. Is your life going to be smooth sailing? The answer is NO, but it can be easier and not so frightening. Your life will be guided and protected in that warm embrace that will help you take that next step. Each step will draw you closer to what God wants for your life. God's plan for your life is perfect. Run to Him and embrace it!

What of that child that is lost and not knowing which way to her home? Who will guide this little lost lamb to safety? You're screaming to yourself, "Please don't let the wolves attack her in the woods. Let her be safe and warm in the arms of her mommy and daddy…"

What about you? Do you feel like this little child? Daddy (God) is waiting for you. He will lead you up the staircase of your life. This means that even in those tough times when it seems like you will be destroyed, God's assurance of being with and guiding you is ALWAYS there. Just reach out and take His hand.

Remember that God says, ✞*"Don't panic. I'm with you. There's no need to fear for I'm your God. I'll give you strength. I'll help you. I'll hold you steady, and keep a firm grip on you."*

✞Psalm 119:104 (The Message)
✞John 8:12 (The Message)
✞Jude 1:2 (The Message)
✞Isaiah 41:10 (The Message)

Karen Anderson's *Soaring To Hope* website is full of inspiration and encouragement to help you rise above life's storms. Find information about her as an inspirational speaker, mentor, and author. Follow her on Facebook.

Inspirational Videos
Video clips of Karen's former TV shows "Move Our Mountains":

www.youtube.com:
Acct Name: kafaithclimber

Karen's Other Writings
The Bible Study, "Life Lessons from God's Golden Girl" is Her other books include, Nikki's Tail-Waggin' Lessons, and The Little Book of BIG Thoughts Series.

Contact Information: Karen Anderson
Soaring To Hope
Website: www.soaringtohope.com/contacts
and leave your message or questions.
****

PERMISSIONS
Scriptures taken from The Message
Copyright 1993, 1994, 1995, 1996, 2000, 2001, 2002.
Used by permission of NavPress Publishing Group
Scriptures taken from the HOLY BIBLE & NEW INTERNATIONAL
Copyright 1973, 1978, 1984 by International Bible Society
Used by permission of Zondervan. All Rights Reserved
Scriptures taken from the NEW KINGS JAMES version.
Copyright 1982 by Thomas Nelson, Inc.
Used by permission. All Rights Reserved

Made in the USA
Middletown, DE
18 September 2024

60561085R00047